# 809 Creative Chicken Names

## FROM TRADITIONAL, ECCENTRIC, AND FUNNY ALL THE WAY TO MODERATELY INAPPROPRIATE: UP YOUR CHICKEN-NAMING GAME WITH THIS HELPFUL COMPILATION

### LM TAYLOR

# Introduction

Welcome to the wonderful world of chicken names! Naming your feathered friends is a fun and exciting way to express your creativity and add personality to your flock. Whether you have a few chickens in your backyard or a whole coop full, finding the perfect names can be a delightful challenge and is one of the most fun chicken activities of all poultry-related tasks. In this book, you'll discover 809 suggestions and ideas to inspire your chicken-naming adventure. Names are categorized into Chapters for more accessible selection. We've got traditional, all kinds of funny, classic, eccentric, goofy, "punny," and some bordering on offensive – there is something here for every Crazy Chicken Lady, and every chicken!

Every Crazy Chicken Lady, and every chicken has a unique personality and distinct characteristics. Sometimes people name their chickens based on physical traits like color, feather pattern, or size. Some earn their names from their personality, disposition, or a particular quirk. One Magnificent Crazy Chicken Lady I know has a particularly "rough" looking rooster she calls Keith Richards. Perfection. Another has named a good portion of her flock after the cast of one of her favorite TV shows. I've got one that likes to chase cows for some reason. Her name is Cow Dog.

But not everyone goes for the funny or sarcastic angle – you could just as easily choose classic leading ladies; Greta Garbo, Elizabeth Taylor or Sofia Loren. Or stick with puns – Feather Locklear, Chick Norris, Tu-Peck. The list goes on – so let's get cracking and find the perfect name for your cluckers!

## CHAPTER 1
# Traditional

---

Do not count your chickens before they are hatched.

— AESOP

---

Why did the chick cross the road?
To get to the other side.

- Mrs./Miss/Mr. Peckers
- Chicken Little
- Tweety
- Foghorn Leghorn
- Woodstock
- Fluffy
- Puffy
- Waddles
- Diva
- Pecky

- Heihei
- Lady Kluck
- Ginger
- Torchic
- Alan-a-dale
- Miss Prissy
- Sheldon
- Panchito Pistoles
- Babs
- Chickaletta
- Ernie the Giant Chicken
- Roy Rooster
- Fowler
- Chanticleer
- Robot Chicken
- Buck Cluck
- Clara Cluck
- Runt of the Litter
- Goldie
- Blondie
- Sunny
- Raven
- Cotton
- Snow
- Chocolate
- Vanilla
- Strawberry
- Butterscotch
- Caramel
- Cinnamon
- Honey

- Salty
- Sweet
- Sour
- Bitter
- Shadow
- Midnight
- Chickie Chickie
- Cluck Cluck
- Eggbert
- Gertrude McFuzz
- Peckov
- Cluckov
- Chickov
- Roosterofsky
- Chickovsky
- Angry Bird

CHAPTER 2

# *A Little Bit Country...*

CHICKEN SONGS:

The Chicken In Black – Johnny Cash
Chicken Fried – Zac Brown Band
Dixie Chicken – Little Feat
Sic 'Em On A Chicken – Zac Brown Band
Chicken Train – The Ozark Mountain Daredevils

- Boots
- Lasso
- Barb Wire
- Cowboy Coffee
- Horseshoe
- Hoof Pick / Hoof "Peck"
- Spurs
- Tom Sawyer
- Huck Finn
- Davy Crocket

- Daniel Boone
- James Bowie
- Wild Bill Hickock
- Calamity Jane
- Annie Oakley
- Belle Starr
- Pearl Hart
- Buffalo Bill
- Billy the Kid
- Wyatt Earp
- Doc Holiday
- Sam Bass
- Dale Earnhardt
- Dale Jarrett
- Daryll Waltrip
- Michael Waltip
- Dick Trickle
- Clint Eastwood / "Cluck" Eastwood
- Bonanza
- John Wayne / The Duke
- Rooster Cogburn
- Big Jake
- Tonto
- The Long Ranger
- Miss Kitty
- Chester
- Zorro
- Aunt Bea
- Barney Fife
- Opie
- Katie Elder

- Laura Engels
- Mr. Ed
- Howdie Doodie
- Merle Haggard
- Waylon Jennings
- Buck Owens
- Hank Williams
- Johnny Cash
- Georg Strait
- Willie Nelson
- Porter Wagner
- Conway Twitty
- Garth Brooks
- Rodney "Cockington" Carrington
- Urban Cowboy
- Rhinestone Cowboy
- Dolly Parton
- Tammy Wynette
- Loretta Lynn
- Reba McEntire
- Shania Twain
- Faith Hill
- Kelly Clarkson / Kelly "Cluck"-son
- Tanya Tucker / Tanya "Clucker"
- Teri Clark / Teri "Cluck"
- Crystal Gale
- Patsy Cline
- Pam Tillis
- Lorrie Morgan
- The Judds (Wynona, Ashley, Naomi)
- Elvira

- Huckleberry
- Mustang Sally
- Casey Tibbs
- Larry Mahan
- Jim Shoulders
- Ty Murray
- Roy Duval
- Does your chicken chase cows? Cattle Guard, Wrangler, or Cow Dog.

# CHAPTER 3

# A Little Bit Rock 'n' Roll...

Life was just a tire swing... Blackberry pickin', eatin' fried chicken.

— JIMMY BUFFET

CHICKEN SONGS:

Ain't Nobody Here but Us Chickens – Louis Jordan
Chicken Farm – Dead Kennedys
5-Piece Chicken Dinner – Beastie Boys

- Elvis
- Jerry Lee Lewis
- Freddy Mercury
- Cher
- Madonna

- Tina Turner
- Joni Mitchell
- ACDC
- Quiet Riot
- Fleetwood Mac
- Creedence Clearwater Revival
- Joan Jett
- Cyndi Lauper
- Slash
- Sting
- David Bowie / David "Crowie"
- Mick Jagger / "Chick Jagger"
- Ozzy Osbourne
- Melissa Etheridge
- Iggy Pop
- Stevie Nicks
- Janis Joplin
- Kurt Cobain
- Courtney Love
- Chuck Berry
- Pat Benatar
- Keith Richards
- Alice Cooper
- James Hetfield
- Axl Rose
- Janice Joplin
- Steven Tyler
- Rock-a-bye-Billie
- Olivia Newton John

# CHAPTER 4

# Thug Life / Hip Hop / R&B

---

Mmm...Fried chicken, fly vixen /

Give me heart disease but need you in my kitchen

— NAS

---

## CHICKEN SONGS:

Do the Funky Chicken – Rufus Thomas
I Move Chickens – Gucci Mane

- TuPac / "Tu-Peck"
- Notorious B.I.G. / Biggie Smalls
- P Diddy / Puff Daddy / Puffy "Combs"
- Snoop Dogg
- Busta Rhymes
- Dr. Dre

- Ice Cube
- Wu-Tang Clan
- Jay-Z
- 50 Cent
- Sir Mix-A-Lot / Sir Chicks-A-Lot / Sir Clucks-A-Lot / Sir Crows-A-Lot
- Vanilla Ice
- MC Hammer
- Kanye
- Beyonce (Destiny's Child)
- Kelly Rowland (Destiny's Child)
- Michelle Williams (Destiny's Child)
- Lisa "Left Eye" Lopez (TLC)
- Tionne "T-Boz" Watkins (TLC)
- Rozonda "Chilli" Thomas (TLC)
- Mary J Blige
- Missy Elliott
- Lauryn Hill
- Queen Latifah
- Foxy Brown
- Lil' Kim
- Cardi B
- Nicki Minaj
- Lizzo

# CHAPTER 5

# More Female Vocal Powerhouses

---

Eat fried chicken every day, as the angels go sailing by.

— ELLA FITZGERALD

---

- Aretha Franklin
- Etta James
- Ella Fitzgerald
- Billie Holiday
- Nina Simone
- Carole King
- Donna Summer
- Diana Ross
- Karen Carpenter
- Barbara Streisand
- Annie Lennox
- Gladys Knight
- Amy Winehouse

- Celine Dion
- Mariah Carey
- Whitney Houston
- Christina Aguilera
- Brittany Spears
- Lady Gaga
- Adele

# CHAPTER 6

# Overly Aggressive Roosters

---

I have a painting where somebody's holding a chicken, and underneath the chicken is somebody's head.

— JEAN-MICHEL BASQUIAT

---

Why don't chickens like people?
They beat eggs.

- Trouble
- The Plague / Bubonic
- Lucifer / "Roocifer"
- Scarface
- Vito Corleone
- Michael Vick
- Harvey Weinstein
- Bill Cosby
- Jeffrey Epstein

- Prince Geoffrey
- OJ Simpson
- Charlie Manson
- John Wayne Gacy
- Ted Bundy
- Jefferey Dahmer
- David Berkowitz
- Hannibal Lecter
- Bianchi and Buono
- Richard Ramirez
- HH Holmes
- Jack the Ripper
- Buffalo Bill
- Pablo Escobar
- Hitler
- Osama Bin Laden
- Ivan the Terrible
- Vlad the Impaler
- Benito Mussolini
- Joseph Stalin
- Vladimir Putin
- Muammar Gaddafi
- Kim Jong-un

# CHAPTER 7
## *Violent Hens*

---

"When your mama was the geek, my dreamlets", Papa would say, "she made the nipping off of noggins such a crystal mystery that the hens themselves yearned toward her, waltzing around her, hypnotized with longing."

— KATHERINE DUNN

---

- Susan Atkins
- Attila the Hen
- Morgan le Fay
- Miranda Priestly
- Wednesday Addams
- Veruca Salt
- Mommy Dearest
- Mama Fratelli
- Norma Bates

- Annabelle
- Madam Mim
- Carrie
- Calypso
- Delores Claiborne
- Annie Wilkes
- Ghislaine Maxwell
- Lizzie Borden
- Bloody Mary
- Aileen Wuornos
- Red Sparrow
- Red Queen
- Daenerys
- Cersei Lannister
- Tanya Harding
- Hela
- Firestarter
- Maleficent

# CHAPTER 8
## For the Fighters

What did the counsellor say to the egg?
Say no to crack.

- Muhammad Ali
- Joe Frazer
- Cassius Clay
- Rocky "Cocky" Balboa
- Apollo Creed
- Ivan Drago
- John Wick
- Bruce Lee
- Undertaker
- Birdzilla
- Beth Dutton
- Bellatrix Lestrange
- Harley Quinn
- Ellen Ripley
- Furiosa
- Daenerys Targaryen

- Khaleesi
- Arya Stark
- Cruella de Vil
- The Scarlet Witch
- Nebula
- Poison Ivy
- Queen
- Wicked Witch of the West
- Alien Queen
- Nurse Ratched
- Medusa
- Lady Macbeth
- Lady Tremaine

# CHAPTER 9

# So Wrong...But So Right...

---

I was eating in a Chinese restaurant downtown. There was a dish called Mother and Child Reunion. It's chicken and eggs. And I said, I gotta use that one.

— PAUL SIMON

---

- Breakfast
- Yoko Ono / "Yolko" Ono
- John Denver Omelet
- Consuela Spanish Omelet
- Over Easy
- Poached
- Braised
- Eggo
- Bacon and Eggs
- Hard Boiled
- Soft Boiled

- Deviled
- Salmonella
- Chick-Fil-A
- Boneless
- Piccata
- Sesame
- Hollandaise
- Frittata
- Parmesan
- Noodle
- Barbie Q
- Original Recipe
- Extra Crispy
- Drum Stick
- Hot Wing
- Rotisserie
- Peking Duck
- Dark Meat
- White Meat
- Chicken Nugget
- Stuffin'
- Brunch
- Quiche
- Soup
- Pot Pie
- Fried Steak
- Enchilada

## CHAPTER 10

# *Just Because I Think These are Funny*

---

A Jewish woman had two chickens. One got sick, so
the woman made chicken soup out of the other one to
help the sick one get well.

— HENNY YOUNGMAN

---

- Pox
- Ugly Duckling
- Hammock
- Tighty Whitey
- Thong
- Brisket
- Piglet
- Kitten
- Tadpole
- Catfish
- Cheeseburger

- Muffin
- Pickle
- Lunchmeat
- Taco
- Turducken
- Kung Pao
- Bugs Bunny
- Yosemite Sam
- Hot Tamale
- Flip Flop
- Slippers
- High Heel
- Stiletto
- Rubber Boots
- Birkenstock
- Bullwinkle
- Elmo
- Cat Lady
- Lester Holt
- Tom Brokaw
- Walter Cronkite
- Diane Sawyer
- Katie Couric
- Barbara Walters
- William Dafoe
- Jeff Goldblum
- Jim Carry
- Rick Moranis
- Got a fast chicken? How about Secretariat, or Sea Biscuit? Speedy Gonzales? Too Obvious. Run DMC - better.

- Donkey Kong
- Hulk Hogan
- Rowdy Roddy Piper
- Maybe I Should Get Bangs
- I Should Start a Pod Cast
- Business in Front, Party in the Back
- Superhero Landing
- Negasonic Teenage Warhead
- The Real Housewives of [enter your house/town/farm here]
- The Pope
- The Girl with the Chicken [or Rooster] Tattoo
- Cool Runnings
- I'm Still Going To Use Someone Else's Netflix
- Or just...Netflix
- Hulu
- Peacock

# CHAPTER 11
## More For Roosters

Why did the rooster never come home to his hen at night?
He was free range.

- Alarm Clock
- Noise Machine
- Noise Maker
- Big Daddy
- Mr. Big
- Colonel Sanders
- Russel "Crowe"
- Tank
- Chuck Norris / "Cluck" Norris / "Chick" Norris
- Mr. T
- Johnny Bravo
- Rico Suave
- Weird Al
- Boy Georg
- Crackhead Carl
- Frankie Doodle Doo

- Lenny "Crow"-vtiz
- "Cluck" Kent
- Kung Fu
- Pecker
- James Bond
- General Tso
- Punky Rooster
- Franklin Delano "Roostervelt"
- Mr. Rogers
- The Big Lebowski / The Dude
- Big Bootie Rudy
- Cock-a-doodle-DON'T
- Barry Mani-"crow"
- "Roo" Hefner
- "Roo" Paul
- Luke "Combs"
- Shawshank
- Stephen King
- Quentin Tarantino
- David Hasselhoff

\* \* \*

**If you are enjoying this book, please consider leaving a review.**

\* \* \*

# CHAPTER 12
## Adult Theme

What happens when hens and roosters get together?
It's eggciting.

Why did the chicken cross the road, roll in the mud, and cross again?
Because it was a dirty double crosser.

- Hanky Panky
- Poker in the Front
- Dirty Duck
- Peeping Tom
- John Holmes
- Ron Jeremy / The Hedgehog
- Captain Cock
- Mrs. Pull It
- Mother Clucker
- Cluck It
- What the Cluck
- Cluck Off

- BBC – Big Black Chicken
- Jezebel
- Pink Lady
- Half Baked
- Dazed and Confused
- Pineapple Express
- Drunk and Disorderly
- Drunk in Public

Ever had a Rooster that turned out to be a Hen? How about:

- Bruce "Henner"
- A Rooster Named Sue

# CHAPTER 13

# Duos, Trios, and Ensembles

> We can see a thousand miracles around us every day. What is more supernatural than an egg yolk turning into a chicken?
>
> — S. PARKES CADMAN

- Thelma and Louise
- Elsa and Ana
- Maverick and Goose
- Ann and Nancy Wilson
- Smokey and The Bandit
- Smith and Wesson
- Hannibal Lector and Clarice Starling
- Ike and Tina Turner
- Brad Pitt and Angelina Jolie
- Mickey and Minnie
- Mario and Luigi

- Bonnie and Clyde
- Salt-n-Pepa
- Bill and Ted
- Bert and Ernie
- Beavis and Butthead
- Wayne and Garth
- Jack, Janet, and Chrissy
- Harry, Ron and Hermione
- Buffy, Willow, and Xander
- Captain Kirk, Spock, and McCoy
- Larry, Curly, and Moe
- Chevy Chase, Steve Martin, and Martin Short
- Farrah Fawcett, Jaclyn Smith, and Kate Jackson
- Blossom, Bubbles, and Buttercup
- Judy, Violet and Doralee
- Ferris, Cameron, and Sloane
- Alvin, Simon, Theodore
- Shrek, Fiona, and Donkey
- Snap, Crackle, and Pop
- Frank Sinatra, Dean Martin, and Sammy Davis Jr.
- Carrie, Samantha, Charlotte, and Miranda
- Dorothy, Blanche, Rose and Sofia
- John Lennon, Paul McCartney, Ringo Starr, George Harrison
- Stan, Kyle, Cartman, and Kenny
- Tootie, Blair, Natalie, Jo, and Mrs. Garrett
- Jerry, Kramer, Elaine, Costanza, Newman
- Scary Spice, Sporty Spice, Baby Spice, Ginger Spice, Posh Spice
- Dopey, Doc, Bashful, Sneezy, Happy, Grumpy and Sleepy

- Hank, Peggy and Bobbi Hill, Luanne Platter, John Redcorn, Boomhower, Bill, and Dale
- Charlie Brown, Linus, Lucy, Peppermint Patty, Sally, Schroeder, Franklin, Marcie, Pig-Pen, Woodstock, Snoopy
- Sam Malone, Woody Boyd, Diane Chambers, Rebecca Howe, Carla Tortelli, Norm Peterson, Cliff Clavin, Frasier Crane, Lilith Sternin

# CHAPTER 14

# Inspired by our Favorite Adult Beverages

---

Did you really just compare me to chicken wings?

You say that like it's a bad thing. Chicken wings are the bomb.

— JULIE JAMES

---

- Whisky
- Whiskey River
- Whiskey Ditch
- White Lightning
- Sangria
- Margarita
- Mojito
- Black & Tan
- Rum & Coke
- Hooch

- Hoot Wine
- Chardonnay
- Merlot
- Moonshine
- Gin & Tonic
- Vodka Tonic
- Colorado Bulldog
- Fuzzy Navel
- Fish Bowl
- Harvey Wallbanger
- Duck Fart
- Monkey Gland
- Fluffy Critter
- Dirty Shirley
- Alabama Slammer
- Rusty Nail
- Lemon Drop
- Coors
- PBR
- Schlitz
- Olympia
- Hamms
- Dr. Pepper / Dr. "Pecker"

# CHAPTER 15
## *Historical*

---

Boys, I many not know much, but I know chicken poop from chicken salad.

— LYNDON B. JOHNSON

---

- Eleanor Roosevelt
- Franklin D. Roosevelt
- Georg Washington
- John Hancock
- Thomas Jefferson
- John Adams
- Abraham Lincoln
- Betsy Ross
- Hamilton
- Benjamin Franklin
- Paul Revere

- Thomas Edison
- John D. Rockefeller
- Henry Ford
- Susan B. Anthony

# CHAPTER 16

# Based on Games

---

Ginger: Listen. We'll either die free chickens or we die trying.

Babs: Are those the only choices?

— CHICKEN RUN

---

- Badminton
- Lawn Dart
- Parcheesi
- Battleship
- Checkers
- Cribbage
- Cricket
- Tag
- Kick The Can
- Cornhole

- Croquet
- Shuffleboard
- Hopscotch
- Roblox
- Minecraft
- Fortnite
- Grand Theft Auto

# CHAPTER 17
# Literary Great and Inspiring Artists

---

I don't know which is more discouraging, literature or chickens.

— E.B. WHITE

---

- Angie Dickinson
- Harriet Beecher Stowe
- Jane Austen
- Virginia Woolf
- Mary Shelley
- Emily Bronte
- Agatha Christie / "Eggatha" Christie
- JK Rowling
- Harper Lee
- Charlotte Bronte
- Gertrude Stein
- Angela Lansbury

- Emily Dickinson
- Edgar Allen Poe / "Eggdar" Allen Poe
- Picasso
- Vincent van Gogh
- Leonardo da Vinci
- Michelangelo
- Andy Warhol
- Georgia O'Keefe
- Jackson Pollock
- Mona Lisa

# CHAPTER 18
## Sports Greats

---

Rocky: Now, the most important thing is, we have to work as a team, which means: you do everything I tell you.

Fetcher: Birds of a feather flop together.

— CHICKEN RUN

---

- Larry "Bird"
- Magic Johnson
- Michael Jordan
- Dennis Rodman
- Bill Russel
- Kareem Abdul-Jabarr
- Wayne Gretzky
- Phil Mickelson
- Tiger Woods

- Arnold Palmer
- Jerry Rice
- Jim Brown
- Walter Payton
- Barry Sanders
- Joe Greene
- Tom Brady
- Peyton Manning
- Brett Farve
- Johnny Unitas
- Terry Bradshaw
- Joe Montana
- John Elway
- Dan Marino
- Joe Namath
- Brian "The Boz" Bosworth
- Ty Cobb
- Babe Ruth
- Nolan Ryan
- Shoeless Joe Jackson
- Pete Rose
- Ken Griffey Jr.
- Roberto Clemente
- Sandy Koufax
- Rogers Clemens
- Derek Jeter
- Pele
- Flo Jo
- Roger Federer
- Steffi Graf
- Serena Williams

- Billie Jean King
- Martina Navratilova
- Katie Ledecky
- Mary Lou Retton
- Nadia Comaneci
- Dorothy Hamill
- Kristi Yamaguchi
- Tara Lipinski
- Michelle Kwan
- Danica Patrick
- Lisa Leslie

# CHAPTER 19
## Strong Female Personalities

---

Nick: Yeah, but you've got to get the chicken first to get the egg, and then you get the egg to get the chicken out of.

Fetcher: Hang on. Let's go over this again?

— CHICKEN RUN

---

- Frida Kahlo
- Ruth Bader Ginsburg
- Maya Angelou
- Katherine Hepburn
- Oprah
- Nancy Pelosi
- Mary Queen of Scots
- Elizabeth I
- Rosa Parks

- Marie Curie
- Virginia Woolf
- Margaret Thatcher
- Celie Harris Johnson
- Amelia Earhart
- Princess Diana
- Katherine Johnson
- Jane Goodall
- Ruth Handler
- Hillary Clinton
- Toni Morrison
- Ellen DeGeneres
- Gloria Steinem
- Susan B Anthony
- Estee Lauder
- Florence Nightingale
- Helen Keller
- Cleopatra
- Sacajawea
- Mother Teresa
- Betty Crocker
- Julia Child
- Martha Stuart

# CHAPTER 20
## Female Leads

---

I'll change you from a rooster to a hen with one shot!

— DOLLY PARTON, 9 TO 5

---

- Betty White
- Elizabeth Taylor
- Ingrid Bergman
- Tippy Hedren / "Chicky Hen-dren")
- Bette Davis
- Meryl Streep / Meryl "Cheep"
- Anjelica Huston
- Greta Garbo
- Marlene Dietrich
- Jean Harlow
- Grace Kelly
- Judy Garland
- Liza Minelli

- Lauren Bacall
- Hedy Lamarr
- Sophia Loren
- Joan Crawford
- Marilyn Monroe
- Audrey Hepburn
- Lucille Ball
- Carol Burnette
- Gilda Radner
- Wanda Sykes
- Annie Potts
- Darryl Hannah
- Shirley MacLaine
- Sissy Spacek
- Diane Keaton
- Mia Farrow
- Goldie Hawn
- Jamie Lee Curtis
- Jane Fonda
- Lily Tomlin
- Dolly Parton
- Bette Mildler
- Sally Field
- Sigourney Weaver
- Geena Davis
- Whoopi Goldberg
- Pamela Anderson
- Jennifer Aniston / "Henifer" Aniston
- Heather Locklear / "Feather" Locklear
- Gwyneth Paltrow / Gwyneth "Poultry"

# CHAPTER 21

# Fashion Icons and Luxury Cars

---

Ace: Are you ready to rock?

Hollywood Runt: Ain't no mountain high enough. Ain't no valley low.

— CHICKEN LITTLE

---

- Gucci
- Versace
- Dior
- Prada
- Burberry
- Chanel
- Louis Vuitton
- Giorgio Armani
- Calvin Klein
- Valentino

- Hubert de Givenchy
- Vera Wang
- Oscar de la Renta
- Jimmy Choo
- Manolo Blahnik
- Christian Louboutin
- Armani
- Rolex
- Tiffany
- Swarovski

Name your flock after these icons – then, if you're sarcastic )
(like me), name "that one chicken":

- Kmart
- Walmart
- Dollar Store
- Salvation Army
- Costco
- Target
- Kohl's
- TJ Maxx
- Old Navy
- Gap
- Forever 21
- Timex

## LUXURY VEHICLES

- Porsche

- Ferrari
- Mercedes
- Bentley
- BMW
- Maserati
- Lamborghini
- Cadillac
- Aston Martin
- Lexus
- Jaguar
- Roll-Royce
- Lincoln
- Bugatti
- Audi

Less than Luxury Brands/Models:

- POS
- Kia
- Hyundai
- Honda
- Impala
- Chevy Chevette
- Ford Taurus
- Ford Pinto
- VW Bug

## CHAPTER 22
## Fictional Characters

---

We all like chicken.

— MALCOLM X

---

- Buckbeak
- Jean-Luc "Peckhard" aka The Captain
- Nancy Drew
- Indiana Jones
- Magnum PI
- Bart Simpson
- Alf
- Mary Poppins / Mary "Poopins"
- Urkel
- Punky Brewster
- Pretty Woman
- Scarlett O'Hara
- Maria Von Trapp

- Jackie Brown
- Erin Brockovich
- Elle Woods
- Jessica Rabbit
- Ariel
- Hermione Granger
- Harry Potter
- Voldemort
- Rasputin
- Katniss Everdeen
- Abominable
- Yeti
- Loch Ness
- Princess Leia / Princess "Lay-a"
- Luke Skywalker
- Hans Solo
- Jabba the Hut
- Baby Yoda
- Mandalorian
- Darth Vader
- Jar Jar Binks
- Lara Croft
- Leeloo
- Mulan
- Sarah Conner
- Terminator
- Black Widow
- Trinity
- Neo
- Aeon Flux
- Ursula

- Bilbo Baggins
- Gandalf / Gandalf the Grey
- Frodo
- Legolas
- Aragorn
- Galadriel
- Smaug

\* \* \*

**If you enjoyed this book, please consider leaving a review.**

\* \* \*

# Bibliography

*9 to 5*. Directed by Colin Higgins, 20th Century Studios, 19 Dec. 1980.

"100 Best Chicken Quotes, Sayings and Phrases | Kidadl." *Kidadl.com*, kidadl.com/quotes/best-chicken-quotes-sayings-and-phrases.

"A Quote by Lyndon B. Johnson." *Www.goodreads.com*, www.goodreads.com/quotes/85046-i-may-not-know-much-but-i-know-chicken-shit. Accessed 13 June 2023.

Beastie Boys. *5-Piece Chicken Dinner*. 1989.

Buffett, Jimmy. *Life Is Just a Tire Swing*. 1974.

Cash, Johnny. *The Chicken in Black*. 1998.

*Chicken Little*. Directed by Mark Dindal, Walt Disney Pictures, Walt Disney Studios Motion Pictures, 30 Oct. 2005.

"Chicken Quotes." *BrainyQuote*, www.brainyquote.com/topics/chicken-quotes.

*Chicken Run*. Directed by Nick Park and Peter Lord, DreamWorks Pictures, Pathé, Universal Pictures, 20th Century Studios, 20th Century Home Entertainment, 8 Dec. 2000.

Dead Kennedys. *Chicken Farm*. 1985.

Dunn, Katherine. *Geek Love*. London, Abacus, 2015.

Finn, Amy. "120 Chicken Quotes to Make You Appreciate Them." *Www.quoteambition.com*, 22 July 2021, www.quoteambition.com/chicken-quotes/.

---. "120 Chicken Quotes to Make You Appreciate Them." *Www.quoteambition.com*, 22 July 2021, www.quoteambition.com/chicken-quotes/.

Fitzgerald, Ella. *Cabin in the Sky*. 1940.

Gucci Mane. *I Move Chickens*. 2007.

"Henny Youngman Quotes." *BrainyQuote*, www.brainyquote.com/quotes/henny_youngman_106841. Accessed 12 June 2023.

James, Julie. *About That Night*. Penguin, 3 Apr. 2012.

"Jean-Michel Basquiat Quotes." *BrainyQuote*, www.brainyquote.com/quotes/jeanmichel_basquiat_543053. Accessed 13 June 2023.

Jordan, Louis . *Ain't Nobody Here but Us Chickens*. 1956.

Little Feat. *Dixie Chicken*. 1973.

Nas. *Fried Chicken*. 2008.

"Paul Simon Quotes." *BrainyQuote*, www.brainyquote.com/quotes/paul_simon_312941. Accessed 12 June 2023.

The Ozark Mountain Daredevils. *Chicken Train*. 1980.

Thomas, Rufus. *Do the Funky Chicken*. 1970.

X, Malcolm, and Alex Haley. *The Autobiography of Malcolm X*. 1965. New York, Ballantine Books, 2015.

Zac Brown Band. *Chicken Fried*. 2005.

---. *Sic 'Em on a Chicken*. 2006.